CREATIVE TOUCHES™

Wall Finishes
ETC.

D1410898

THE HOME DECORATING INSTITUTE®

COWLES
Creative Publishing
A Division of Cowles Enthusiast Media, Inc.

CONTENTS

Getting Started

Painted Finishes

Special Effects

Wall Finishes
ETC.

Wall surfaces in the home often stand unnoticed as the silent partners in a decorating scheme. With a variety of attention-drawing treatments and finishes, however, they can be given a more prominent place in the overall look of the room.

Several painted finishes, suitable for walls or cabinets, can create very distinctive looks. Select a sleek enamel paint finish for a light-reflective, space-expanding appearance on cabinets and woodwork. Or, acquire an aged look with a crackled paint finish. For an elegant wall, apply a painted finish that resembles silk moiré.

Wall surfaces can be dramatized by some special effects, such as wall frame moldings. Upholstered walls are a warm, soft alternative to paint or wallcovering. Fabric-draped walls are a unique way to add softness and texture, without permanent commitment. Specialized painting techniques, including faux mosaic and hand-painted or stenciled trompe l'oeil, offer ways to showcase your artistic talent.

You no longer have to settle for understated walls. Let the colorful photography and detailed instructions on these pages help you transform your walls into active elements in your decorating plan.

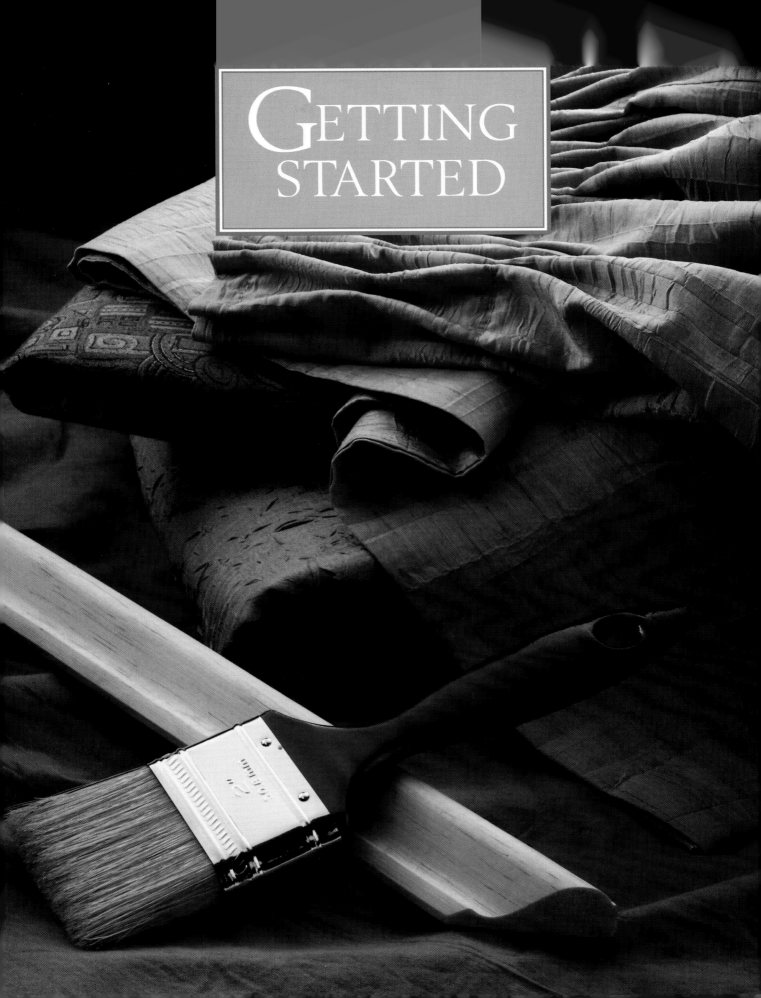

GETTING STARTED

Preparing the Surface

To achieve a high-quality and long-lasting paint finish that adheres well to the surface, it is important to prepare the surface properly so it is clean and smooth. The preparation steps vary, depending on the type of surface you are painting. Often it is necessary to apply a primer to the surface before painting it.

PREPARING SURFACES FOR PAINTING

SURFACE TO BE PAINTED	PREPARATION STEPS	PRIMER
UNFINISHED WOOD	1. Sand surface to smooth it. 2. Wipe with damp cloth to remove grit. 3. Apply primer.	Latex enamel undercoat.
PREVIOUSLY PAINTED WOOD	1. Clean surface to remove any grease and dirt. 2. Rinse with clear water; allow to dry. 3. Sand surface lightly to degloss and smooth it and to remove any loose paint chips. 4. Wipe with damp cloth to remove grit. 5. Apply primer to any areas of bare wood.	Not necessary, except to touch up areas of bare wood; then use latex enamel undercoat.
PREVIOUSLY VARNISHED WOOD	1. Clean surface to remove any grease and dirt. 2. Rinse with clear water; allow to dry. 3. Sand surface to degloss it. 4. Wipe with damp cloth to remove grit. 5. Apply primer.	Latex enamel undercoat.
UNFINSHED WALLBOARD	1. Dust with hand broom, or vacuum with soft brush attachment. 2. Apply primer.	Flat latex primer.
PREVIOUSLY PAINTED WALLBOARD	1. Clean surface to remove any grease and dirt. 2. Rinse with clear water; allow to dry. 3. Apply primer, only if making a dramatic color change.	Not necessary, except when painting over dark or strong color; then use flat latex primer.
UNPAINTED PLASTER	1. Sand any flat surfaces as necessary. 2. Dust with hand broom, or vacuum with soft brush attachment.	Polyvinyl acrylic primer.
PREVIOUSLY PAINTED PLASTER	1. Clean surface to remove any grease and dirt. 2. Rinse with clear water; allow to dry thoroughly. 3. Fill any cracks with spackling compound. 4. Sand surface to degloss it.	Not necessary, except when painting over dark or strong color; then use polyvinyl acrylic primer.
UNGLAZED POTTERY	1. Dust with brush, or vacuum with soft brush attachment. 2. Apply primer.	Polyvinyl acrylic primer or gesso.
GLAZED POTTERY, CERAMIC & GLASS	1. Clean surface to remove any grease and dirt. 2. Rinse with clear water; allow to dry thoroughly. 3. Apply primer.	Stain-killing primer.
METAL	1. Clean surface with vinegar or lacquer thinner to remove any grease and dirt. 2. Sand surface to degloss it and to remove any rust. 3. Wipe with damp cloth to remove grit. 4. Apply primer.	Rust-inhibiting latex metal primer.
FABRIC	1. Prewash fabric without fabric softener to remove any sizing, if fabric is washable. 2. Press fabric as necessary.	None.

Tools & Supplies

TAPES

When painting, use tape to mask off any surrounding areas. Several brands are available, varying in the amount of tack, how well they release from the surface without damaging the base coat, and how long they can remain in place before removal. You may want to test the tape before applying it to the entire project. The edge of the tape should be sealed tightly to prevent seepage.

PAINT ROLLERS

Paint rollers are used to paint an area quickly with an even coat of paint. Roller pads, available in several nap thicknesses, are used in conjunction with roller frames. Use synthetic or lamb's wool roller pads to apply water-based paints.

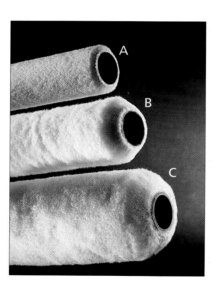

A. SHORT-NAP ROLLER PADS with ¼" to ⅜" (6 mm to 1 cm) nap are used for applying glossy paints to smooth surfaces like wallboard, wood, and smooth plaster.

B. MEDIUM-NAP ROLLER PADS with ½" to ¾" (1.3 to 2 cm) nap are used as all-purpose pads. They give flat surfaces a slight texture.

C. LONG-NAP ROLLER PADS with 1" to 1¼" (2.5 to 3.2 cm) nap are used to cover textured areas in fewer passes.

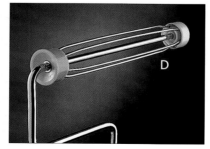

D. ROLLER FRAME is the metal arm and handle that holds the roller pad in place. A wire cage supports the pad in the middle. Select a roller frame with nylon bearings so it will roll smoothly and a threaded end on the handle so you can attach an extension pole.

E. EXTENSION POLE has a threaded end that screws into the handle of a roller frame. Use an extension pole when painting ceilings, high wall areas, and floors.

PAINTBRUSHES & APPLICATORS

Several types of paintbrushes and applicators are available, designed for various purposes. Select the correct one to achieve the best quality in the paint finish.

A. SYNTHETIC-BRISTLE paintbrushes are generally used with water-based latex and acrylic paints, while B. NATURAL-BRISTLE brushes are used with alkyd, or oil-based paints. Natural-bristle paintbrushes may be used with water-based paints to create certain decorative effects.

C. BRUSH COMBS remove dried or stubborn paint particles from paintbrushes and align the bristles so they dry properly. To use a brush comb, hold the brush in a stream of water as you pull the comb several times through the bristles from the base to the tips. Use mild soap on the brush, if necessary, and rinse well. The curved side of the tool can be used to remove paint from the roller pad.

Stencil brushes are available in a range of sizes. Use the small brushes for fine detail work in small stencil openings, and the large brushes for larger openings. Either D. SNYTHETIC or E. NATURAL-BRISTLE stencil brushes may be used with acrylic paints.

Artist's brushes are available in several types, including F. FAN, G. LINER, and H. FLAT BRUSHES. After cleaning the brushes, always reshape the head of the brush by stroking the bristles with your fingers. Store artist's brushes upright on their handles or lying flat so there is no pressure on the bristles.

I. SPONGE APPLICATORS are used for a smooth application of paint on flat surfaces.

J. PAINT EDGERS with guide wheels are used to apply paint next to moldings, ceilings, and corners. The guide wheels can be adjusted for proper alignment of the paint pad.

Water-based Paints & Conditioner

A wide variety of paint is available from paint supply stores and craft stores. Each type has advantages that make it especially suitable for certain kinds of painting. All of the following are water-based, making cleanup easy with soap and water. Water-based paints are also safer for the environment than oil-based paints.

LATEX PAINTS

Latex paint is fast drying and durable. In addition to the wide range of premixed colors, latex paint can be custom-mixed by a paint professional. It is available in various finishes, from flat latex for a matte appearance to high-gloss latex with maximum sheen. Low-luster latex enamel paint, sometimes referred to as eggshell enamel, has some sheen and provides good coverage; semigloss has a bit more sheen. The glossier the paint, the more durable it is. Packaged in pints, quarts, and gallons (0.5, 0.9, and 3.8 L), latex paint is suitable for general use in small and large jobs.

Latex paint contains acrylic or vinyl resins or a combination of both. Latex paints of acrylic resins are the highest quality, with vinyl-acrylic blends next in quality, followed by paints consisting solely of vinyl resins. High-quality paints may cost significantly more, but they provide an even, complete coverage and wear longer.

CRAFT ACRYLIC PAINT

Craft acrylic paint contains 100 percent acrylic resins. Generally sold in 2-oz., 4-oz., and 8-oz. (59, 119, and 237 mL) bottles or jars, these premixed acrylics have a creamy brushing consistency and give excellent coverage. They should not be confused with the thicker artist's acrylics used for canvas paintings. Craft acrylic paint can be diluted with water, acrylic extender, or latex paint conditioner if a thinner consistency is desired. Craft acrylic paints are available in many colors and in metallic, fluorescent, and iridescent formulas.

LATEX PAINT CONDITIONER, such as Floetrol®, was developed for use in a paint sprayer with latex paint, but this useful product is also essential in making paint glaze for faux finishes. When paint conditioner is added to paint, it increases the drying or "open" time without affecting the color. The mixture has a lighter consistency and produces a translucent paint finish. Latex paint conditioner may be added directly to either latex or acrylic paint.

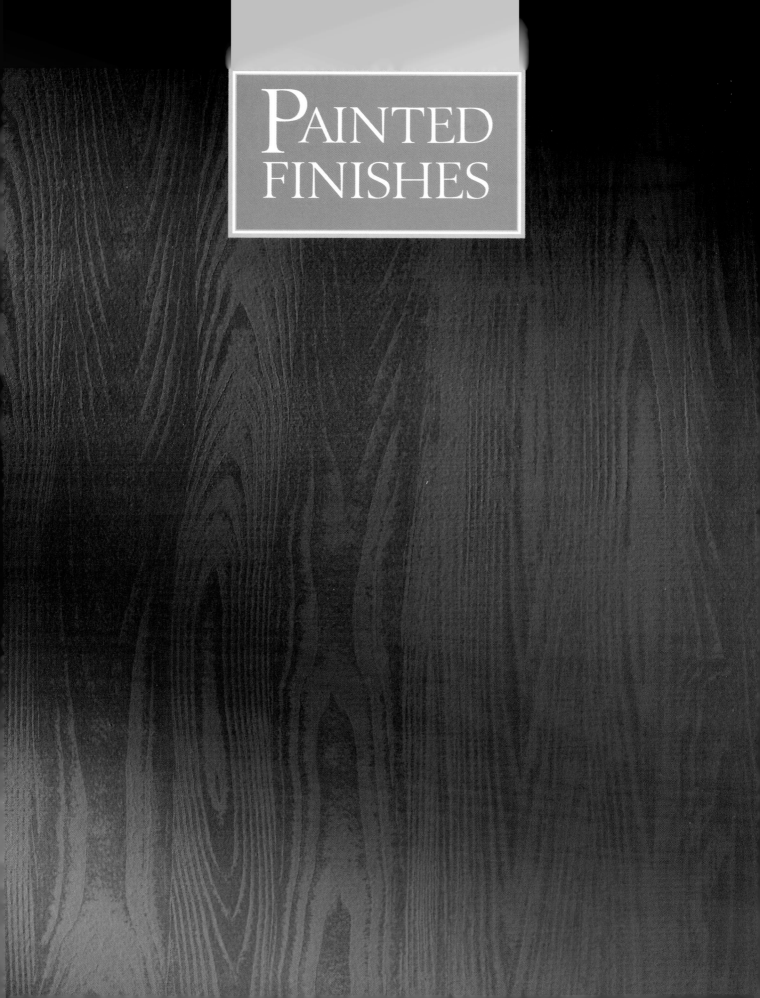

PAINTED FINISHES

Enamel Paint Finish

The timeless look of white painted cabinets is appropriate for any decorating style. With the use of good equipment and high-quality paint, you can achieve a professional-looking finish on most wood types, depending on the grain of the wood.

The enamel paint may be applied with a high-quality paintbrush. However, for best results when painting large areas like cabinet doors and drawer fronts, it is recommended that the paint be applied with a sprayer. The use of a sprayer prevents any brush strokes or ridges caused by a paintbrush, paint roller, or sponge applicator.

There are two main types of paint sprayers: airless and air. Although airless sprayers are known to clog and apply paint unevenly, air sprayers perform with excellent results.

The air sprayers are a commercial grade of sprayer referred to as LPHV, meaning low pressure and high volume. Available from rental stores, they apply paint in an even coat without clogging and with minimal overspray. They are easy to use, even for do-it-yourselfers. The width of the spray area and the amount of the paint that is released are adjustable. Because the operation instructions may vary somewhat from one brand to another, practice on a large sheet of cardboard until you are accustomed to using the sprayer and have the spray flow properly adjusted. After each use, clean the sprayer according to the manufacturer's instructions.

Use a high-gloss latex enamel paint for a durable, smooth finish. For a smooth application, dilute the paint with a latex paint conditioner, according to the manufacturer's instructions. The ratio of paint to conditioner varies, depending on whether a sprayer or paintbrush is used. Dilute only the amount of paint that you intend to use in a day, and use the same ratio each day. Before applying the paint, prepare the wood surface as on page 9.

How to apply an enamel paint finish

MATERIALS

- High-gloss latex enamel paint.
- Latex paint conditioner, such as Floetrol®.
- LPHV air paint sprayer, available from rental stores.
- High-quality synthetic paintbrush.
- 220-grit sandpaper.
- Tack cloth.

1. Unscrew the doorknobs and drawer pulls; remove cabinet doors and drawers. Prepare all wood surfaces (page 9). Mask off any surfaces that are not to be painted.

2. Fill air sprayer according to manufacturer's instructions. Practice painting on large sheet of cardboard, adjusting spray flow for a smooth, light application of paint with no runs.

3. Spray the cabinet doors and drawer fronts in a clean, well-ventilated area, applying light coat of paint. Clean the sprayer. Allow paint to dry for 8 hours.

4. Paint cabinet interiors and edges of cabinets, using paintbrush; allow to dry for 8 hours. Apply additional coats of paint as necessary.

5. Repeat step 3 to apply at least three light coats of paint, allowing each coat to dry for 8 hours. Paint back sides of the doors after the door fronts are thoroughly dry, using a sprayer or paintbrush.

6. Secure the doorknobs and drawer pulls when the paint is thoroughly dry. Hang cabinet doors.

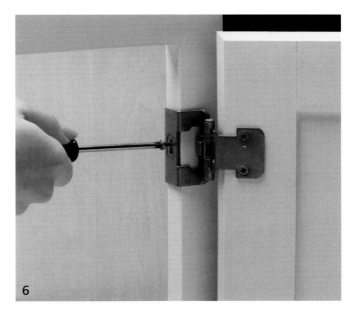

Crackled Finish

This paint finish transforms wooden kitchen cabinets, furniture, and accessories into pieces with the timeworn look of antiques. Crackling, a technique developed in response to the increasing appeal of aged furnishings, uses contemporary products to imitate the effects of aging and weathering on paint. A crackled finish can be applied to unfinished wood or previously varnished or painted wood.

A base color of paint is applied to a prepared wood surface, followed first by a crackle medium, then by a top coat of paint in a second color. Almost instantly, the crackle medium causes the top coat of paint to crackle randomly, revealing the base color. To give an even more aged appearance, artist's oil paints can be rubbed randomly onto the crackled surface. A clear acrylic finish is applied as a final coat for durability.

Acrylic and latex paints can be successfully crackled; be consistent in using either acrylic or latex paint for the base coat and the top coat. Because the composition of paints varies from brand to brand, some paints may not crackle as desired. Test the products on a scrap of lumber before working on the actual project, varying the length of time the crackle medium sets before the top coat of paint is applied. The thickness of the top coat can also change the look of the crackling. Because the crackle medium may tend to run, apply it horizontally whenever possible.

For a prominent crackling effect, select light and dark contrasting paint colors. For the optional artist's oil paints, select a color similar to the base coat to mix with a gray or brown. This gives a muted effect that is compatible with the color of the crackling.

How to apply a crackled finish

MATERIALS

- ◆ Paint in two colors for base coat and top coat; paintbrush.
- ◆ Crackle medium, such as Quick-Crackle™.
- ◆ Artist's oil paints in two colors, selected as described on page 21, optional.
- ◆ 220-grit sandpaper
- ◆ Clear acrylic finish.

1. Prepare wood surface (page 9). Apply a base coat of paint in desired color to the wood surface. Allow to dry.

2. Apply even, light coat of crackle medium over the base coat. Allow to set for length of time specified by the manufacturer or according to your own test results for desired crackling effect. For a large project, such as a cabinet, work on a limited area at a time, so you do not exceed setting time.

3. Apply paint in a contrasting color; paint will crackle soon after it is applied. Allow top coat to dry.

4. Give crackled finish a more aged appearance, if desired, by mixing two artist's oil paints together. Rub small amounts of mixed oil paint onto the crackled surface, following wood grain; reapply until the desired effect is achieved. If too much oil paint is applied to an area, remove excess by sanding lightly with 220-grit sandpaper; wipe sanded surface with tack cloth.

5. Apply one or two coats of clear acrylic finish, for added durability.

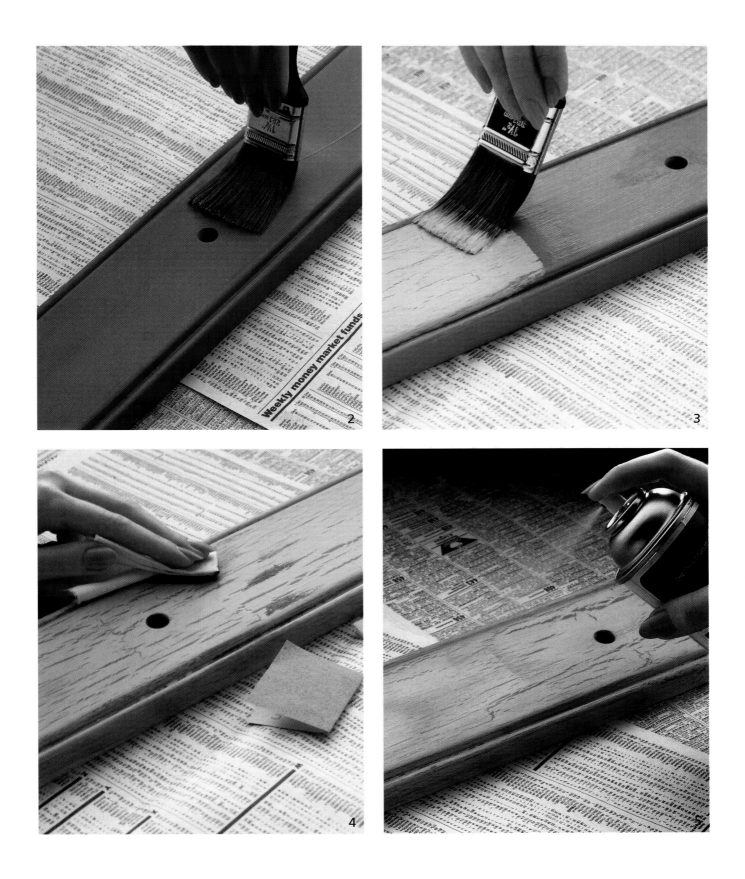

Faux Moiré

For the watermarked look of silk moiré fabric, use a process similar to the wood-graining technique of faux wood. The subtle tone-on-tone pattern can be created in any color for a coordinated decorating scheme. This finish is recommended for small areas, such as below a chair rail or within frame moldings.

A rocker tool designed for wood graining is used for this watermarked effect. A paint glaze (page 26) is applied over a base coat of paint, and the graining tool is pulled and rocked through the glaze to create impressions. Then a dry paintbrush is pulled across the markings to mimic the crosswise grain of moiré.

The glaze used for faux moiré contains more paint than most glazes, making it thicker and more opaque. In order to finish the graining before the glaze has dried, apply the glaze to a small area at a time. If faux moiré is used on the wall area below a chair rail or border, work from the chair rail to the baseboard in 12″ (30.5 cm) sections, working quickly.

Moiré is simulated by using a darker shade for the base coat and a lighter glaze for the top coat. This gives the brighter sheen that is characteristic of moiré fabric.

How to apply a faux moiré paint finish

MATERIALS

- Low-luster latex enamel paint in darker shade, for base coat.
- Low-luster enamel paint in lighter shade, for glaze; or base-coat paint, lightened with white paint, may be used.
- Latex paint conditioner, such as Floetrol®.
- Wood-graining rocker.
- Paint roller or paintbrush, for applying the base coat and the glaze.
- Natural-bristle paintbrush, 2" to 3" (5 to 7.5 cm) wide, for dry brushing.

FAUX MOIRÉ GLAZE

Mix together the following ingredients:

Two parts semigloss latex enamel paint.

One part latex paint conditioner.

One part water.

1. Prepare surface and apply base coat of low-luster latex enamel. Allow to dry.

2. Mix glaze. Apply an even coat of glaze over a base coat to a small area at a time, rolling or brushing vertically.

3. Slide graining tool vertically through wet glaze, occasionally rocking it slowly back and forth, to create watermarked effect. Start at one corner, working in one continuous motion as you slide and rock the tool from one end to another. As you rock the tool, oval markings are created.

4. Repeat step 3 for subsequent rows; stagger the oval markings, and work quickly before glaze dries. Wipe the excess glaze from tool as necessary.

5. Pull dry brush horizontally across surface when glaze has partially dried, using a natural-bristle paintbrush; this mimics the crosswise grain of the moiré fabric. Wipe excess glaze from the brush as necessary. Allow paint to dry.

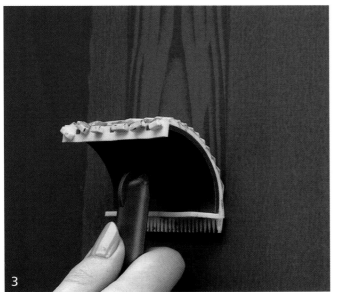

SPECIAL EFFECTS

Faux Mosaic

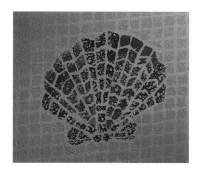

Simulate a mosaic design with a painting technique that uses small pieces of sponge as stamps. For easier handling, several pieces of sponge are glued to a small piece of foam board, allowing you to create intricate stamped designs in a single printing. Make a separate stamp for each mosaic design and each color because the stamps cannot be cleaned. If the project is not finished in one day, used stamps may be kept overnight in tightly sealed plastic bags.

Faux mosaic works for smooth or textured surfaces. Use it to create a border design along the ceiling, to frame a window or archway, or to embellish the wall below a chair rail. Or use faux mosaic on accessories like vases and planter stands.

Before you start painting, you may want to sketch the mosaic design to scale on graph paper as shown on page 33.

MATERIALS

- Flat or low-luster latex paint, for base coat.
- Latex or craft acrylic paints in desired colors, for mosaic design.
- Cellulose sponges; slightly dampened sponges are easier to use.
- Pieces of foam board; craft glue; disposable plates; artist's eraser.
- Utility knife or razor blade; ruler.
- Carpenter's level, for marking walls.
- Transparent Mylar® sheets and painter's masking tape.

How to make the stamps for a mosaic design

1. Cut the cellulose sponge into ¾″ (2 cm) squares or other mosaic shapes, using a utility knife.

2. Cut piece of foam board with a utility knife, to be used as a base for the stamp. For an overall grid design, cut 2″×2″ (5 × 5 cm) base to hold four ¾″ (2 cm) sponge squares. For a straight-line design, cut 1″×4″ (2.5 × 10 cm) base to hold four sponges. For small details, cut a 1″×1″ (2.5×2.5 cm) base to hold one sponge.

3. Glue sponges of same height to base, spacing them about ⅛″ (3 mm) apart. To keep mosaic design irregular in appearance, do not space sponges precisely. Allow glue to dry.

4. Make stamps for mosaic motifs by cutting desired shape from foam board, for base. Cut the sponges into desired shapes to fill the design area; glue pieces to base, spacing them about ⅛″ (3 mm) apart. Allow glue to dry.

How to paint a faux mosaic design

1. Measure area to be painted with mosaic design. Make diagram of the area on graph paper, drawing the mosaic design to scale on the diagram, using colored pencils; include any details such as motifs or borders.

2. Apply base coat to wall in the desired color; use a mortar color for base coat, for the look of real grout. Allow to dry.

Continued

How to paint a faux mosaic design
(CONTINUED)

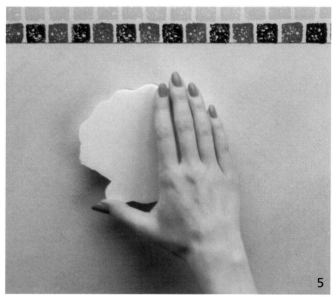

3. Mark outer guidelines of the design area lightly on base-coated surface, using a pencil; to mark walls, use carpenter's level. Mark any other significant placement lines, such as dividing lines, borders, and motifs.

4. Pour small amount of latex or craft acrylic paint in each color for mosaic stamps onto disposable plates. Dip stamp lightly into paint for a one-color stamp (A). Or apply paint colors to individual pieces of sponge (B). Blot onto paper to remove excess paint.

5. Stamp the mosaic design onto surface, using marked lines as a guide, stamping any dividing lines, borders, and motifs; reapply paint to the stamp as necessary. Use a separate stamp for each mosaic design and color combination.

6. Cut Mylar® for each motif, ⅛" (3 mm) larger on all sides. Secure folded painter's masking tape to back of Mylar. Mask off stamped motifs by securing Mylar to the surface over the motif.

7. Finish stamping background area. When stamping the area surrounding motifs, allow the stamps to overlap the Mylar. Allow paint to dry.

8. Remove the Mylar from motif areas. Erase any marked lines that are not covered with paint, using artist's eraser.

Wall Frame Moldings

Add architectural detail to a living room by installing molding in a picture-type frame on the walls. Frame molding can be used to accent special features of the room, divide large walls into smaller sections, and add interest to otherwise plain walls. The molding may be the same color as the walls or a contrasting color. The effect can be intensified by painting the wall area within the frame molding a different color or by wallpapering it.

Crown moldings and chair rail moldings, available in a variety of styles, work well. To determine the size and location of the frames, cut strips of paper the width of the molding and experiment with different frame sizes, taping the strips to the wall. Frame molding often repeats the size of architectural details in a room, such as the width of the windows or fireplace.

Install the molding with small finish nails near the outside corners of the molding and at wall stud locations; use nails long enough to go through the wall surface and into the studs. If wall studs are not located, apply small dots of wood glue to the back of the molding to prevent the frame from pulling away from the wall.

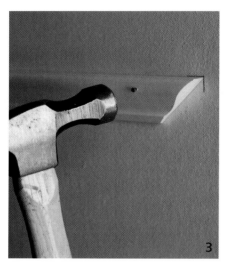

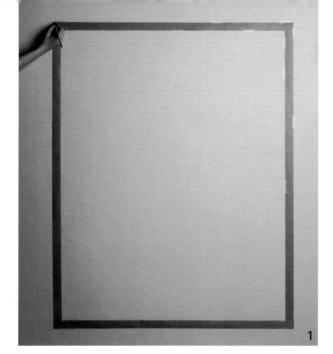

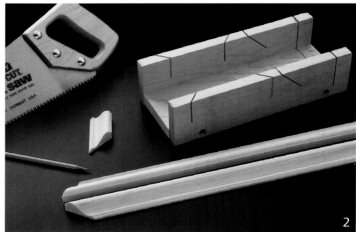

MATERIALS

- Wood molding.
- Miter box and backsaw, or power miter saw.
- Finish nails; nail set.
- Drill; 1/16" (1.5 mm) drill bit.
- Wood glue, if necessary.
- Paint, or wood stain and putty to match stain.

1. Cut paper strips to width of the molding; secure to wall, using tape. Lightly mark the placement for outer edge of the upper molding with a pencil, making sure markings are level.

2. Measure and mark length of upper and lower molding strips on outer edge; cut molding strips, using a miter box and backsaw and angling cuts in from the mark. Check to see that the molding strips are exactly the same length. Repeat to cut the side strips.

3. Paint or stain the moldings. Predrill nail holes with 1/16" (1.5 mm) drill bit. Position upper molding strip on wall, aligning it with markings; if molding will not be nailed to studs, place dots of glue sparingly on back of molding. Nail the moldings to the wall, leaving nails slightly raised.

4. Attach molding strips for sides of the frame, placing a nail at upper corners only. Attach lower strip, making sure the frame is square. Secure remaining nails for sides of the frame.

5. Countersink the nails, using nail set. Touch up nail holes and mitered corners with paint, or fill them with putty to match the stain.

More ideas for wall frame moldings

ABOVE, LEFT: FRAMED AREA is wallpapered, dividing an otherwise plain wall.

ABOVE, RIGHT: DOUBLE MOLDING is used to further emphasize the architectural detailing.

LEFT: CONTRASTING MOLDING calls special attention to the artwork in this traditional grouping.

Fabric-draped Walls

Give your walls a soft, sound-absorbing treatment with draped fabric panels. These unlined fabric panels are constructed with a facing at the upper edge. If desired, the facing can be cut from contrasting fabric and folded to the front of the panel for a banded effect. The facing strip should have a finished width of 1" (2.5 cm) or wider if a contrasting band is desired.

Hang the panels, using decorative cord (left) or fabric tabs (pages 42 and 43), from a series of knobs or decorative hooks. Decorative knobs are available in many styles and finishes. Some styles include screws suitable for inserting into woodwork. Other knobs, intended for use with a bolt, can be secured to woodwork or drywall using hanger bolts (page 42), available at specialty woodworking stores. Knobs are generally mounted 4" to 10" (10 to 25.5 cm) apart, depending on the amount of drape desired.

CUTTING DIRECTIONS

Determine the desired finished length of the drape from the top of the facing to the bottom of the hem. Cut the fabric with the length equal to the finished length plus 2½" (6.5 cm). The total cut width of the fabric after seaming is equal to one-and-one-half to two times the desired finished width plus 4" (10 cm).

Determine the desired number of tabs or cords for the drape, spacing them 6" to 12" (15 to 30.5 cm) apart, depending on the amount of fullness desired. If fabric tabs are desired, cut two 1¼" (3.2 cm) strips of fabric for each tab to the necessary measurement plus ½" (1.3 cm) for seam allowances.

Cut the facing strip twice the desired width plus 1" (2.5 cm). The cut length of the facing strip is equal to the cut width of the panel; piece strips together as necessary.

MATERIALS

- Lightweight to mediumweight decorator fabric.
- Decorative knobs or hooks.
- Hanger bolts, if necessary for securing knobs to woodwork.

DECORATIVE KNOBS that have screws with a wood thread at one end are suitable for inserting into woodwork. Knobs that have screws without a wood thread (A) can be made suitable for inserting into woodwork by replacing the screw with a hanger bolt (B). Hanger bolts have a metal thread at one end for inserting into the knob and a wood thread at the opposite end for inserting into the woodwork. Use appropriate anchors if installing hanger bolts into drywall.

How to sew tabbed fabric panels

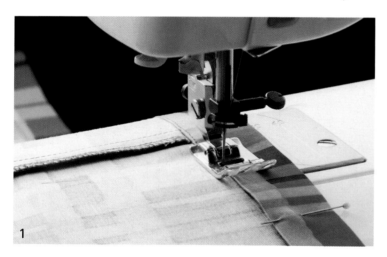

1. Stitch fabric widths together for each panel, stitching ½" (1.3 cm) seams. Finish the seams. At lower edge of the panel, press under 1" (2.5 cm) twice to wrong side of panel; stitch, using straight stitch or blind-stitch, to make double-fold hem.

2. Place two tab strips right sides together, matching raw edges. Stitch ¼" (6 mm) seam on long edges. Repeat for remaining tabs. Turn tabs right side out, and press.

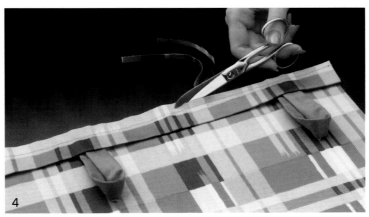

3. Fold tabs in half. Pin to upper edge of panel, matching raw edges. Pin tabs to right side of panel if facing will be folded to wrong side; pin tabs to wrong side of panel if facing will be folded to right side for contrasting band. Place tabs at ends 2″ (5 cm) from each side; space remaining tabs evenly between end tabs. Machine-baste tabs in place.

4. Fold the facing strip in half lengthwise, wrong sides together; press. Pin the facing to right side of panel at upper edge, matching raw edges; or, for contrasting band, pin to wrong side of panel. Stitch 1/2″ (1.3 cm) seam at upper edge; trim to 1/4″ (6 mm).

5. Press the facing to wrong side of panel; or for contrasting band, press the band to right side. Topstitch close to upper edge and folded edge of facing or band.

6. Press under 1″ (2.5 cm) twice at the sides. Stitch to make double-fold hems, using a straight stitch or blindstitch.

7. Hang the panel from knobs or from decorative hooks.

Upholstered Walls

Upholstered walls help create an inviting atmosphere. The fabric covers any imperfections on the walls, and the batting, used as padding, helps insulate the room and absorbs sound. Avoid using fabrics in plaids or stripes, because they call attention to walls that are not squared. Stapling the fabric to drywall or paneled walls is easy; however, staples will not penetrate metal corner pieces. For plaster walls, check to see if staples will penetrate the wall and hold. Before starting, remove switch plates and outlet covers. Do not remove moldings or baseboards, because double welting will cover the fabric edges.

CUTTING DIRECTIONS

Cut fabric lengths as figured in the chart on page 46; do not trim the selvages unless they show through the fabric. Measure around doors and windows and along the ceiling and baseboard; also measure from the floor to the ceiling at each corner. For the double welting, cut fabric strips, 3" (7.5 cm) wide, equal to the total of these measurements.

MATERIALS

- Decorator fabric; polyester upholstery batting.
- Staple gun and 3/8" to 1/2" (1 to 1.3 cm) staples; pushpins; single-edged razor blades; hot glue gun and glue sticks; thick craft glue.

WORKSHEET FOR CALCULATING FABRIC

Cut Length	in. (cm)	
Measurement from floor to ceiling plus 3″ (7.5 cm)*	=	
Cut Width		
Width of fabric minus selvages	=	
Number of Fabric Widths Needed for Each Wall		
Width of wall	=	
Divided by cut width of fabric	÷	
Number of fabric widths for wall**	=	
Amount of Fabric Needed for Double Welting		
Total welting length (see Cutting Directions)	=	
Divided by cut width of fabric	÷	
Number of strips**	=	
Multiplied by 3″ (7.5 cm)	×	
Fabric needed for double welting	=	
Total Fabric Needed		
Cut length (figured above)	=	
Number of fabric widths (figured above) for all walls	×	
Fabric needed for all walls	=	
Fabric needed for double welting	+	
Total length needed	=	
Divided by 36″ (100 cm)	÷	
Number of yd. (m) needed	=	yd. (m)

*Allow extra for pattern repeat; do not subtract for windows and doors unless they cover most of the wall.

**Round up to the nearest whole number.

How to match a patterned fabric

1. Position fabric widths, right sides together, matching selvages. Fold back the upper selvage until pattern matches; lightly press foldline.

2. Unfold selvage; pin fabric widths together on foldline. Check match from right side.

3. Repin fabric widths so pins are perpendicular to the foldline; stitch on the foldline, using a straight stitch. Trim the fabric to finished length.

How to upholster a wall

1. Staple batting to wall every 6″ (15 cm), leaving a 1″ (2.5 cm) gap between batting and the edge of ceiling, corners, baseboard, and moldings. Butt edges between widths of batting. Cut out batting around switch and outlet openings.

2. Stitch the fabric panels together for each wall separately, matching pattern (page 47), if necessary. Plan seam placement to avoid seams next to windows and doors. Make double welting (page 50).

3. Start hanging fabric from the top, turning under ½″ (1.3 cm) and stapling every 3″ to 4″ (7.5 to 10 cm). Begin at a corner where matching is not critical. Do not cut around the windows and doors.

4. Anchor fabric in corners, pulling taut and stapling close to corner so the staples will be covered with double welting. Trim excess fabric. Start next panel at corner.

5. Staple along baseboard, pulling and smoothing the fabric taut to remove any wrinkles. Trim the excess fabric along baseboard, using single-edged razor blade.

6. Mark outside corners of windows and doors with pushpins. Cut out openings with diagonal cuts into corners. Turn under raw edges, and staple around the molding.

7. Apply hot glue to the back of double welting, about 5″ (12.5 cm) at a time; secure the double welting to the upper and lower edges of wall and around window and door frames. Carefully push the double welting in place to cover the staples.

8. Press double welting into corners and around any openings. Use a screwdriver to push double welting into corners. After glue dries, peel off any excess.

9. Apply fabric to switch plates and outlet covers, securing it with diluted craft glue. Clip and trim around openings. Turn raw edges to back of plate; glue in place.

How to make double welting

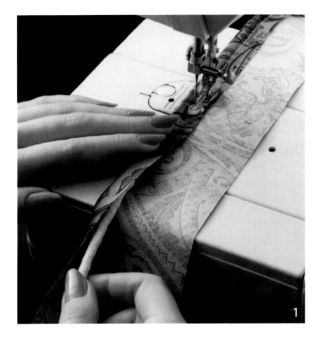

1. Place the cording on wrong side of 3″ (7.5 cm) fabric strip. Fold the fabric over cording, with ½″ (1.3 cm) seam allowance extending. Stitch with the zipper foot next to cording.

2. Place the second cord next to the first cord. Bring the fabric over the second length of cording.

3. Stitch between the two cords on previous stitching line. Trim off excess fabric next to stitching; the raw edge is on the back of finished double welting.

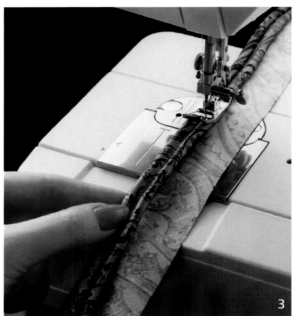

More ideas for fabric on walls

RIGHT: DECORATOR FABRIC is used to upholster the walls above the chair rail. Braid trim is used instead of double welting.

BELOW: BANDED FABRIC PANELS hang from a peg rail. The panels are made following the directions for fabric-draped walls on pages 41 to 43. One-and-one-half times fullness was used.

*H*and-painted *Trompe l'Oeil*

Sophisticated trompe l'oeil murals have the ability to create visual space, almost to the extent that the viewer is tempted to walk into the scene. Such a level of sophistication, obtained by few artists, requires intense study and practice.

There are, however, some simple trompe l'oeil effects that can be successfully achieved with a less skillful hand. The success of the illusion depends on a few basic principles, including scale, perspective, and shading.

SCALE

Objects must be painted the size they would normally appear. Objects look smaller the farther away they are. If an image is to be viewed at close range, it should be painted life-size.

PERSPECTIVE

A sense of depth and distance can be developed by painting images in perspective. In a simple one-point perspective drawing, parallel horizontal lines that run from foreground to background seem to converge at a point on the horizon called the vanishing point.

SHADING

Determine an imaginary light source, and add highlights and shadows to the painted images in reference to that light. For simple trompe l'oeil effects, paint each object in one color tone. Then add highlights by mixing white paint into that color. Paint shadows within the objects by mixing black paint into the original color. Shadows around objects should be painted by mixing black into the original color of the background. It is helpful to study still life photographs to determine the placement of highlights and shadows.

MATERIALS

◆ Drawing paper, pencil, ruler.

◆ Graphite paper.

◆ Craft acrylic paints in desired colors; white paint for mixing highlight colors; black paint for mixing shadow colors.

◆ Artist's brushes, such as a flat shader and a liner.

How to draw an image in one-point perspective

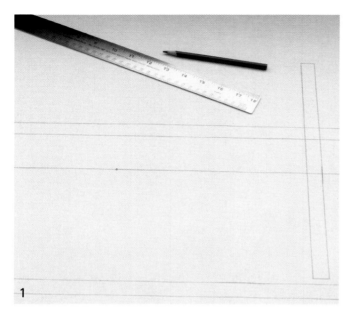

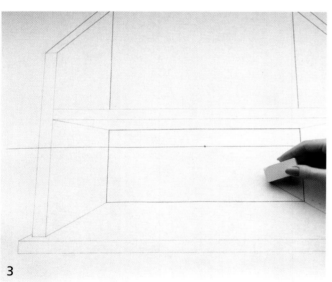

1. Draw a horizontal line (red) across the paper to represent the horizon, or eye level. Draw a point on the horizon to represent vanishing point. Draw to scale primary vertical and horizontal lines (blue) in the foreground, placing horizontal lines a distance above or below the horizon equal to the actual distance they would appear above or below eye level.

2. Draw lines (blue) to represent all parallel horizontal lines that run from the foreground to the background, beginning each line in the foreground and converging all lines at the vanishing point. (Dotted lines show extension of converging parallel lines to vanishing point.)

3. Draw horizontal lines in the background, parallel to horizon line. Draw vertical lines in background. Draw any other connecting lines from foreground to background. Erase unnecessary lines to avoid confusion.

4. Add detail lines and round corners as desired. Erase any unnecessary lines.

How to paint a simple trompe l'oeil image

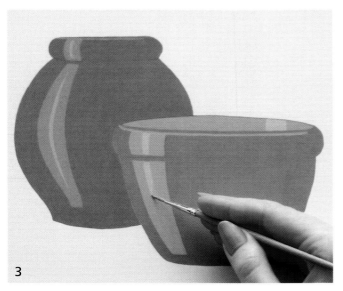

1. Prepare surface (page 9). Apply base coat of the desired color. Allow to dry. Draw the image as in steps 1 to 4, opposite. Or, copy life-size images from magazines. Transfer the image to the surface, using graphite paper.

2. Paint image in single color tones, using desired artist's brushes. Allow to dry. Redraw detail lines.

3. Mix lighter shades of each color, by adding white paint. Paint highlights in areas that would be in direct line with imaginary light source. Allow to dry.

4. Mix darker shades of each color, by adding black paint. Paint shadows that would be created if imaginary light source was shining on image.

*T*rompe l'Oeil *Stenciling*

For people who are less confident of their freehand painting skills or would simply like to try another avenue, a trompe l'oeil effect can be created with stencils. There are some high-quality precut stencils available, with multiple overlays that help the artist create realistic, life-size images. With the use of shading and highlighting techniques, the artist is able to add depth and perspective, giving the stenciled images visual dimension.

Some of the more realistic stencils do not have the bridges, or blank spaces, so common with most stencils. Pinpoint registration marks ensure that each overlay lines up exactly over the preceding one. A pouncing method of application, using craft acrylic paints, allows for successful blending of colors and shading. A wide selection of stencil brushes allows the artist to use a different brush for each paint color, in sizes proportionate to the sizes of the stencil openings. Masking tape wrapped around the bristles 1/4" (6 mm) from the end helps support the bristles during the pouncing motion.

Follow the manufacturer's instructions and color suggestions for completing the stencil, or select color combinations as desired. Several colors may be applied with each overlay, depending on the complexity of the design. Each opening may receive a base color, applied in gradation shading, and then another color for darker shading in areas that would appear in shadow. As with other trompe l'oeil methods, determine an imaginary light source, highlighting foreground areas that would be in direct line with that light source and shading areas that would appear in shadow. After completing the stenciled image, add the shadow that the image would cast on the surface behind it.

MATERIALS

- Precut stencil with multiple overlays.
- Painter's masking tape.
- Craft acrylic paints.
- Stencil brushes.
- Disposable plates; paper towels.

How to stencil a trompe l'oeil image

1. Position the first overlay as desired; secure to the surface, using painter's masking tape. Mark the surface through registration holes, using sharp pencil.

2. Place 1 to 2 tsp. (5 to 10 mL) of paint on disposable plate. Apply masking tape around bristles, ¼" (6 mm) from the end. Dip tip of stencil brush into paint. Using circular motion, blot brush onto folded paper towel until bristles are almost dry.

3. Hold the brush perpendicular to the surface, and apply paint to the first opening, using up-and-down pouncing motion. Apply the paint lightly and evenly throughout the entire opening.

4. Deepen color to desired level by repeated pouncing in areas of the opening that would not be highlighted, shading darker into areas that would appear in shadow; leave highlighted areas pale.

5

6

7

5. Repeat steps 3 and 4 for all openings that receive the same color. Repeat step 2 with the shading color and another brush. Apply shading to areas of openings that would appear in shadow.

6. Repeat steps 2 to 5 for any additional colors on the first overlay. Remove overlay.

7. Position second overlay, aligning registration marks; tape to surface. Repeat steps 2 to 6 for second overlay. Repeat for any subsequent overlays until image is complete.

8. Follow step 2, opposite, using small stencil brush and gray or brown paint. Apply the paint lightly with a pouncing motion along the edges of image opposite light source, simulating shadows.

8

More ideas for trompe l'oeil effects

ABOVE: RAISED PANELS are painted on an interior door, using precut stencils as a guide. Chair rail molding is an illusion created with trompe l'oeil stenciling.

MARK the placement for each panel on door. Move the stencil up or down to complete each panel. Follow the principle of shading (page 53) to determine dark and light areas.

RIGHT: RECESSED NOOK painted in freehand trompe l'oeil invites visitors to take a second look.

BELOW: WINDOW is painted in freehand trompe l'oeil, using one-point perspective (page 53). Stenciled flowers and greens suggest an outdoor flower bed.

Index

A Division of Cowles Enthusiast Media, Inc.

President/COO: Nino Tarantino
Executive V.P./Editor-in-Chief: William B. Jones

Creative Touches™
Group Executive Editor: Zoe A. Graul
Managing Editor: Elaine Johnson
Editor: Linda Neubauer
Associate Creative Director: Lisa Rosenthal
Senior Art Director: Delores Swanson
Art Director: Mark Jacobson
Copy Editor: Janice Cauley
Desktop Publishing Specialist: Laurie Kristensen
Photo Studio Services Manager: Marcia Chambers
Print Production Manager: Patt Sizer

President/COO: Philip L. Penny

WALL FINISHES ETC.
Created by: The Editors of Cowles Creative Publishing, Inc.

Wall finishes etc.
      p. cm. -- (Creative touches)
   Includes index.
   ISBN 0-86573-882-3 (softcover)
   1. House painting -- Amateurs' manuals. 2. Interior decoration -
-Amateurs' manuals. 3. Wall coverings -- Amateurs' manuals.
I. Cowles Creative Publishing. II. Series.
TT323.W3 1997   96-37445
698'. 142 -- dc21   CIP

Books available in the Creative Touches™ series:

*Stenciling Etc., Sponging Etc., Stone Finishes Etc., Valances Etc.,
Painted Designs Etc., Metallic Finishes Etc., Swags Etc.,
Papering Projects Etc., Wall Finishes Etc., Floor Finishes Etc.*

The Creative Touches™ series draws from the individual titles of
The Home Decorating Institute®. Individual titles are also available
from the publisher and in bookstores and fabric stores.

Printed on American paper by:
  R. R. Donnelley & Sons Co.
99 98 97 96 / 5 4 3 2 1

Cowles Creative Publishing, Inc. offers a variety of how-to books.
For information write:
  Cowles Creative Publishing
    Subscriber Books
  5900 Green Oak Drive
  Minnetonka, MN 55343